KU-497-606

Contents

Chapter 1

Is our food safe to eat?

Food provides you with the energy needed for everything you do, and with all the chemicals your body needs to grow, to repair damage and to stay healthy. When you take a mouthful of food, you probably enjoy the taste. Depending what you are eating, you might expect your food to be good for you, too. But what if the food you eat actually makes you ill? If food looks or smells bad, the chances are you won't eat it, but could there be hidden dangers that you cannot detect? We generally take it for granted that our food is safe – but how safe is it really?

Worldwide issues

It is reported that in today's world 854 million people do not have enough to eat and almost 16,000 children die every day from hunger-related causes. In most developed countries, however, there is plenty of food. What worries many people in these countries is not whether they have enough food, but whether the food they do have is safe to eat. While some people are anxious that there might be hidden

These workers are arranging fish fingers into rows at a food processing factory. Today, much of our food is produced in similar factories.

Is Our Food Safe?

Carol Ballard

W

FRANKLIN WATTS
LONDON·SYDNEY

First published in 2008 by Franklin Watts

© 2008 Arcturus Publishing Limited

Franklin Watts
338 Euston Road
London NW1 3BH

Franklin Watts Australia
Level 17/207 Kent Street, Sydney, NSW 2000

Produced by Arcturus Publishing Limited,
26/27 Bickels Yard, 151–153 Bermondsey Street, London SE1 3HA

Series concept: Alex Woolf
Editor: Nicola Barber
Designer: Ian Winton
Illustrator: Stefan Chabluk

Picture credits:
Corbis: cover (Holger Winkler/ zefa), 8, 16 (Sion Touhig), 30 (Lester Lefkowitz), 36 (Jean Pierre Amet/ BelOmbra), 38 (Jim Richardson), 39 (Francois Lenoir/ Reuters), 40 (Gideon Mendel).
Science Photo Library: title page and 35 (Cordelia Molloy), 6 (Maximilian Stock Ltd), 11 and 31 (Peter Menzel), 15 (Chris Knapton), 19 (David Parker), 21 (Scott Sinklier/ AG Stock USA), 22 (Victor de Schwanberg), 23 (Andrew McClenaghan), 24 (Gusto Images), 26 (NIAID/ CDC), 33 (Jane Shemilt), 41 (Philippe Psaila), 43 (Victor Habbick Visions).
Shutterstock: 9 (Supri Suharjoto), 28 (Alan Egginton), 29 (Agphotographer).

Cover: A man wearing a clean suit sprays crops in a greenhouse with pesticide.

A CIP catalogue record for this book is available from the British Library.

Dewey Decimal Classification Number: 363.19'2

ISBN 978 0 7496 8220 0

Printed in China

Franklin Watts is a division of Hachette Children's Books, an Hachette Livre UK company.
www.hachettelivre.co.uk

problems with food, others are happy to accept assurances from governments and producers that food is perfectly safe. Strict regulations cover every aspect of food production, from growing crops and rearing animals through to processing, packaging, storage and sale. There are rigorous standards, and officials check that these standards are maintained.

What are the dangers?
The potential dangers fall into three main categories:

- **genetic modification (GM)** This scientific technique can be used to produce new foods but, despite reassurances from scientists, not everybody is convinced that GM foods are safe.

- **chemicals** These may be added at various stages of food production and processing, and some may not be good for us.

- **microbes** Eating food contaminated by some microbes can cause serious illness.

Ancient to modern
Our ancient ancestors lived on whatever food they could find; they roamed around to hunt animals and to seek out edible plant parts such as fruits, berries and nuts. Over many thousands of years, a gradual change took place. People sowed seeds, tended plants and harvested crops. They domesticated and looked after animals to provide them with milk, eggs and meat.

Early farmers
Early farmers grew what they and their families or social groups needed, relying on native plants and animals that were suited to the environment in which they lived. Gradually, processes of selection began to occur. For example, by choosing to plant seed from only the strongest, healthiest plants, farmers ensured that future generations of plants would be even stronger and healthier.

> ## Expert View
>
> 'An estimated 76 million cases of foodborne disease occur each year in the United States. The great majority of these cases are mild and cause symptoms for only a day or two. Some cases are more serious, and CDC [Centers for Disease Control and Prevention] estimates that there are 325,000 hospitalizations and 5,000 deaths related to foodborne diseases each year.'
>
> **US Department of Health & Human Services, Centers for Disease Control and Prevention website**

They also found ways of storing food so that, even in winter when fresh food was scarce, there was something to eat. Drying, smoking, salting and pickling all helped to preserve food until it was needed.

This photograph from 1939 shows a woman sorting peas in her store room, with the previous year's preserved fruits and vegetables in jars and tins on the shelves and floor around her.

Developing societies

As societies and civilizations developed, farming methods became increasingly organized and sophisticated. Explorers and traders brought new foods from distant lands, expanding the range of foods available. The nineteenth and twentieth centuries were periods of rapid progress. Electricity and machinery speeded up many processes previously done by hand, while steam ships, trains and aeroplanes reduced journey times. Some scientists unravelled the secrets of genetics and inheritance, while others investigated chemicals. They studied microbes and developed ways of combating them. New materials such as plastic were invented and household appliances such as refrigerators and freezers became commonplace. Everyday life was transformed.

FORUM

People hold different views about the merits of traditional versus modern farming methods:

'I believe there is a real and prosperous future for the traditional family farm, in some cases on a more diversified basis – although I know very many farmers have already taken those steps. ... I would be astonished and dismayed if we were to see the disappearance of the traditional family farm.'

Margaret Beckett, UK Environment Secretary, 2001

'There is a need to continue to intensify farming. Organic farming has a place but it will never feed the growing population of the world.'

Professor Bill McKelvey, Head of the Scottish Agricultural College, 2007

Which type of farming do you think offers the best hope for the future?

Modern changes

All these changes have affected the food we eat. Small fields have been combined to make large fields suitable for modern agricultural machinery. Crop yields have been increased through the use of chemicals. Animals are raised in conditions specifically calculated to allow more food to be produced more quickly and in smaller spaces. Chemicals are used to improve the look or taste of food, and to help it last for longer. Organisms can now be changed in laboratories in ways that would once have taken many years of selective breeding. And global transport means that we can have fresh food from anywhere in the world – at any time of year.

Modern science and agriculture, together with air transport, mean that a wide range of fresh fruit and vegetables from all over the world is available in our supermarkets throughout the year.

Chapter 2

What is genetic engineering?

Every living thing is made up of tiny units called cells. Each cell contains a set of instructions, known as its genetic code or genome, which controls everything that happens in the organism. Genetic engineering is a technique that can be used to change the genetic code of a living organism.

Chromosomes and DNA

The genetic information is contained in tiny double-stranded thread-like structures inside the nucleus. These threads are called chromosomes, and each piece of information that they carry is called a gene. Geneticists often visualize the genes lined up along the chromosomes like beads on a necklace. Chromosomes contain a chemical called deoxyribose nucleic acid (DNA) which has a complicated double helix structure, made up from pairs of molecules called bases. There are four bases – adenine (A), cytosine (C), guanine (G) and thymine (T). Each gene is made up of a specific sequence of bases.

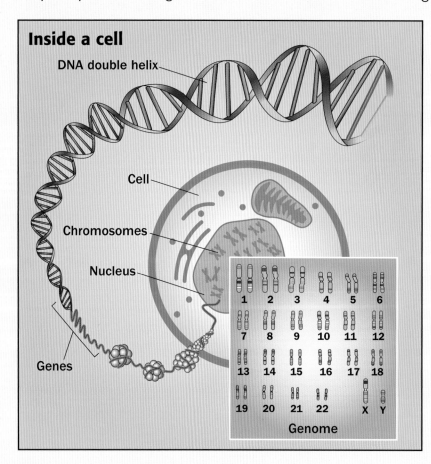

Inside a cell

DNA double helix

Cell

Chromosomes

Nucleus

Genes

1 2 3 4 5 6
7 8 9 10 11 12
13 14 15 16 17 18
19 20 21 22 X Y

Genome

This diagram shows the set of 23 chromosomes that make up the human genome. Each chromosome contains many genes, and each gene is made from linked base pairs of DNA.

Geneticists have worked out the sequence of genes, and the sequence of bases that make up the genes, for many organisms. This means that they know which part of a chromosome carries the gene for a particular characteristic, and exactly what the code is for each gene.

Changing chromosomes

By using enzymes to split a DNA molecule at two precise points, it is possible to remove a gene from a chromosome. Scientists can take a gene from the chromosome of one organism and insert it into the chromosome of another organism. This means that they can transfer a characteristic of one organism into another. This is the basis of genetic engineering. An organism whose genetic code has been changed by genetic engineering is said to have been 'genetically modified', often shortened to GM.

Swapping genes

Genes can be swapped within a species to create new combinations. For example, a gene from a plant variety that produces a few large fruits might be transferred to the genome of a plant from the same variety that produces many small fruits, giving a new variety that produces many large fruits.

These fruits are the result of genetic engineering between plums and apricots. The fruits on the left are apriums and those on the right are pluots.

Genes can be swapped from the genome of one organism into the genome of a very different organism. For example, ordinary tomato plants cannot survive cold weather. To create a tomato that can, scientists looked for an organism that could survive cold conditions. They chose a dogfish, removed the frost-resistant gene from its chromosomes and inserted this gene into tomato plant chromosomes. The resulting organism has all the usual tomato plant characteristics plus the frost-resistant characteristic of the dogfish.

How are GM foods created?

Creating a genetically modified organism is a slow and expensive process. On average it can take between five and ten years and cost as much as US$50 million to US$100 million. First, scientists have to decide which organism they want to modify. This is called the host organism, as it is the one that will receive the new genetic material. Then scientists must identify which characteristic of the host organism they want to modify.

The next step is to identify an organism that has the characteristic the scientists want to transfer to the host. This is called the donor organism, as genetic material will be taken from it. Having found a suitable donor organism, the scientists need to analyse its genome to find the gene or genes that carry the code for the specified characteristic.

FOCUS

GM success

Stuart Armitage and his family began to grow cotton in Australia in 1993. From the beginning, the Armitages had trouble with a pest called corn earworm. They found it difficult and expensive to control the earworm with chemical sprays. In 1999, they switched to a GM variety of cotton called Bollgard II which seems to have solved their problems. Stuart says: "Thanks to Bollgard II cotton we now have a more relaxed family life (no spraying every other night of the week), and I feel good about our pest management practices."

The third step is to extract the gene or genes that carry the code for the required characteristic from the rest of the donor organism's DNA. Enzymes are used to do this, splitting the DNA at very precise points to extract only the section that is needed.

The fourth step is to insert this piece of donor DNA into the host organism. This procedure can be carried out in several different ways, but the oldest and most common method is called recombinant DNA. In this technique the gene is inserted into a ring of DNA, called a plasmid, from a bacterium or virus. The bacterium or virus is then injected into the host cells and the new gene finds its way into the host's DNA. The bacterium or virus thus acts as a carrier, or vector, for the gene that is being transferred into the host.

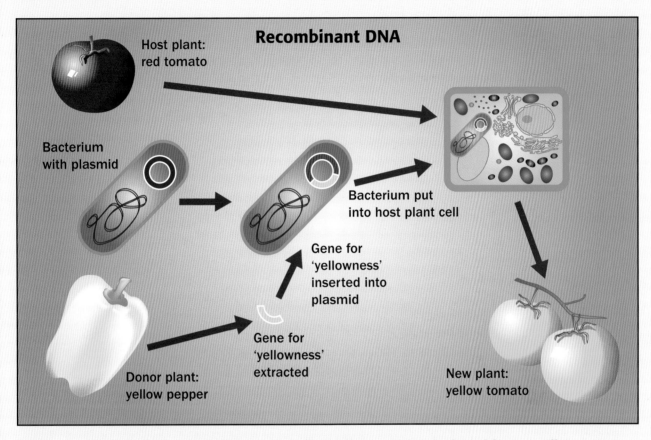

Recombinant DNA

Host plant: red tomato

Bacterium with plasmid

Bacterium put into host plant cell

Gene for 'yellowness' inserted into plasmid

Gene for 'yellowness' extracted

Donor plant: yellow pepper

New plant: yellow tomato

In this example of genetic engineering, a gene for 'yellowness' is transferred from a yellow pepper plant via a bacterium to a red tomato plant. The process creates a new plant that will produce yellow tomatoes.

Once the new gene has been inserted, the host organism can be grown and tested. Scientists check that the new gene has been incorporated into the organism's genome and that the new characteristic is present. Further tests must prove that the organism has not been changed in some other, unexpected way that makes it harmful, dangerous, or less viable than the original. Initial tests are on a small number of organisms in a closely controlled environment. When scientists are sure the organism is safe, larger-scale tests on more organisms can be carried out. Finally, full commercial-scale trials can take place. Once all the testing stages are complete, the organism may be licensed and released for commercial use.

Why are GM foods grown?

GM foods are grown for various reasons. These include:

- **Herbicide resistance** Herbicides can be used to kill weeds – but they also kill the crop plants. Some GM crops are resistant to herbicides, which means that farmers can spray whole fields. One example is a strain of soya bean called Roundup Ready. First planted commercially in 1996, it is resistant to a weedkiller called Roundup. Farmers can plant the beans straight into the soil without clearing the ground of weeds first. They can then spray with Roundup during the growing period, killing the weeds but not damaging the crop.

- **Pest resistance** Some insects can cause serious damage to crop plants. However there is a soil bacterium, *Bacillus thuringiensis*, which releases a toxin that can kill susceptible pests. When the gene for toxin production is transferred into the crop genome, the plant itself produces the toxin. Insects that try to eat the plant will then be killed. This means that the farmer does not need to use pesticides to control crop pests.

- **Disease resistance** Some crops are badly affected by fungal and viral diseases. By creating GM crop plants that are resistant to such diseases, the damage to the crop is reduced.

- **Stress resistance** Plants naturally grow better under some conditions than others. GM crops are being developed that enable a plant to thrive under conditions in which it would normally die or be very weak. This opens up the possibility of growing crops in new places. Current research into *Xerophyta viscosa*, a plant from South Africa, shows that it is extremely good at surviving in drought conditions. Transferring the gene for drought-resistance to a food crop plant might enable food to be grown in arid areas.

- **New characteristics** Using GM techniques, scientists can create crops with new characteristics. One example is 'golden rice'. Ordinary rice is low in the chemicals needed for vitamin A production in the body, so vitamin A deficiency is common in areas where rice is the staple food. Golden rice contains much higher levels of these chemicals and so can help to reduce vitamin A deficiency. Scientists are also working on developing crops that could carry vaccines and other pharmacological chemicals.

The barley in this field has been genetically engineered to produce a higher yield than normal barley. More food can be obtained from the field, so more people can be fed. In countries where there are food shortages, such crops could be very important.

Some plants have been developed that carry more than one of these characteristics. For example, herbicide tolerance and insect resistance can be transferred together to create a herbicide tolerant and insect resistant plant.

Expert View

'The new developments in the area of GM animals ... necessitate a harmonized approach to maintain our current standard for a safe and nutritious food supply in the light of growing numbers of different (GMO-derived) foods and food ingredients and increasingly complex food supply chains.'

Esther J. Kok and Wendelyn Jones
'The food safety risk assessment of GM animals'
(Working paper for the FAO/WHO), 2003

Animals and GM

Although much research into the genetic modification of agricultural animals is being carried out, for example to develop a GM pig that produces leaner meat than a normal pig, or a GM salmon that grows faster and larger than a normal salmon, no GM animal products are currently licensed for human consumption. However, GM crops are used in the production of many animal feedstuffs.

15

Benefits or risks?

Genetic modification is controversial. Some people see it as the answer to many of the world's health and food problems. Others think that we can hardly begin to understand or assess the potential hazards posed by GM techniques because they are still so new. Some regard it as interfering with nature in a way that is against their religious beliefs or ethical standpoint.

Some people are convinced that GM crops are dangerous to humans and to the environment. Here, a group of anti-GM protesters is attempting to destroy a test GM crop.

The potential benefits of genetic engineering in food production have been outlined on pages 14 and 15. The potential risks of genetic engineering include:

• the cross-fertilization of GM plants with native species, possibly damaging the native species in a way that cannot be reversed or controlled.

• interaction with other species that may have a negative effect on the ecosystem as a whole.

- the possibility of causing changes to other characteristics of the organism, making the organism harmful to humans.

- the introduction of different gene mixes into the human food chain, by transferring genes from non-food species into food plants, which may be harmful to human health.

- the possible transfer of allergy from one food to another. For example, the transfer of a gene from a peanut plant into another plant could also transfer the characteristic of the peanut that makes people allergic to it. These people would then be allergic to the new plant as well as to peanuts.

- some GM plants are sterile. This means that farmers cannot save seed from one year to plant in the following year. Instead, they have to buy new seed from the biotech company, which is an extra and possibly unaffordable expense for many poor farmers.

FORUM

People have very different views about the possible benefits and risks of GM food:

'Over the next several years, crop biotechnology will be applied to the development of crops important to the expanding populations of the developing world. In addition, crops with enhanced nutritional properties and even containing vaccines will appear over the next five to ten years. Such products should further enhance consumer acceptance of this new technology.'

Susan K. Harlander, **The Evolution of Modern Agriculture and its Future with Biotechnology,** *2001*

'Technologies for genetically modifying (GM) foods offer dramatic promise for meeting some areas of greatest challenge for the 21st century. Like all new technologies, they also pose some risks, both known and unknown. Controversies surrounding GM foods and crops commonly focus on human and environmental safety, labelling and consumer choice, intellectual property rights, ethics, food security, poverty reduction, and environmental conservation.'

US Department of Energy Office of Science, Human Genome Project

Do the benefits of GM food outweigh the possible risks?

Chapter 3

How do chemicals affect our foods?

Chemicals have been added to fresh foods for hundreds of years. In the days before refrigeration, fresh meat was often stored in barrels of salt water and fresh vegetables were pickled in jars of vinegar. These chemicals helped to preserve the food. In recent years, however, the range of chemicals added to our foods has increased dramatically.

Why are chemicals added to foods?

In the past, individual families or small communities grew, prepared and cooked the food they needed. Now we buy most of our food from shops, and much of it is processed and packaged. Even fresh foods such as vegetables are often wrapped in plastic bags or cartons. As the world's population increases, more people need to be fed so the land has to be more productive. Using chemicals on crops can help to increase the amount of food produced. Chemicals are also used to alter food in various ways. The table shows some of the different types of chemicals that are added, and why they are used.

Production stage	Type of chemical	Reasons for use
Growing crops	Fertilizers	Improve crop growth and yield
	Pesticides	Prevent damage by insects and other pests
	Herbicides	Prevent weed growth
Raising animals	Antibiotics	Prevent illness in animal
	Hormones	Improve growth and quality
During processing	Flavour enhancers	Improve flavour
	Preservative	Increase shelf life
	Colourings	Improve appearance
	Emulsifiers	Improve structure and texture
	Gelling agents	Make product less runny

Mercury alert

Marine biologists have recorded an increase in the levels of some chemicals in fish, especially those at the top of marine food chains such as shark, marlin, swordfish and tuna. One chemical that has caused concern is mercury. High levels of mercury can lead to damage to the brain and nerves, especially in young children and babies. An example is the case of Matthew Davis, a bright and alert ten-year-old from California. When Matthew began to have learning difficulties, his parents became worried and took him to a doctor. Blood tests showed he was suffering from mercury poisoning. Matthew regularly ate white albacore tuna, and this was blamed for his illness. Tuna is an excellent source of many nutrients, but some governments now suggest that people should limit their intake to one or two portions a week.

Healthier foods?

Some chemicals are added to foods to provide extra nutrients. For example, thiamine, a vitamin needed to maintain health, is added to many breakfast cereals. Some eggs are now available with added omega-3 fatty acids, which are thought to help brain activity. Folic acid, a vitamin that helps to prevent nerve defects in newborn babies, is added to some flours and breads.

Accidental additions

Sometimes chemicals get into our food by accident. Chemicals that pollute rivers and seas are ingested by fish. Chemicals from car exhausts are taken up by food crops growing close to busy roads. Accidental contamination of food can occur during its processing at a factory. Wrapping and packaging materials may contain chemicals that can affect the food inside. Even some methods of cooking add chemicals to food – for example, food cooked on a barbecue is likely to pick up chemicals from the smoke.

A researcher investigates the contamination of food by chemicals in its packaging that occurs when the food is cooked in a microwave oven.

Intentional contamination

Occasionally there are news reports about intentional contamination of food at a factory or on supermarket shelves. In most cases, this has been carried out by an individual who wants to cause trouble either for the community or for the business. These incidents are rare, and businesses, supermarkets and authorities act swiftly to minimize any risk to the public from contaminated products.

Chemicals during food production

Plants and animals need nutrients, just as we do, if they are to develop properly and stay healthy. Many chemicals are now available to farmers to help them maximize the growth and yield of their crops and livestock. In the past, some agricultural chemicals were found to be dangerous to human health and their use is now banned in many countries.

Chemicals and crops

There are four main types of chemical that are added to crops:

• **Fertilizers** These contain nutrients needed by a plant to grow and maintain health. Some fertilizers are from natural sources, such as manure or seaweed, while others are man-made mixtures of specific chemicals that are designed to suit a specific type of crop.

Expert View

'The contamination of food by chemical hazards is a worldwide public health concern and is a leading cause of trade problems internationally. Contamination may occur through environmental pollution of the air, water and soil, such as the case with toxic metals, PCBs [polychlorinated biphenyls; chemicals used in some industries] and dioxins [chemicals produced by waste incinerators and chemical plants], or through the intentional use of various chemicals, such as pesticides, animal drugs and other agrochemicals.'

WHO website 'Chemical risks in food'

• **Herbicides** In an open field, seeds from weeds can germinate and grow amongst the crop plants. The weeds take nutrients from the soil, take up space that the crop plants could fill, and make it harder to harvest the crop. Applying herbicides prevents weed growth and so reduces these problems.

• **Pesticides** Slugs, caterpillars, aphids, beetles – a wide variety of pests attack crop plants, causing damage and reducing the yield. Pesticides help to prevent this happening. Some kill pests that touch a treated part of the plant, some are taken up by the plant and kill pests inside the plant.

- *Fungicides* These are used to control and prevent fungal infection in plants. Most fungicides are sprayed or dusted onto growing plants but some are used to treat seeds and soil to prevent the growth of fungal spores.

Chemicals and livestock

Several different types of chemical are available for use in animal husbandry. Regulations governing their use vary, as some chemicals are permitted in some countries but banned in others.

- *Antibiotics* These are used to cure infections, as they are in humans. In some cases, they are given to healthy animals to prevent infection.

- *Vaccines* Vaccination provides an alternative to antibiotics for controlling infectious diseases in farm animals.

- *Hormones* Animals, like humans, produce hormones that regulate their growth. Giving animals extra growth hormones can change their growth patterns to produce larger animals and therefore more food. Hormones given to dairy cattle can increase their milk yield.

- *Pesticides* Animals can suffer from infections by pests such as roundworms. Doses of pesticides can be used to prevent these.

A vet prepares a syringe for the vaccination of pregnant sows in the pens where the pigs are kept to give birth.

Organic farming

Many people are not comfortable with the idea of using chemicals in food production. Organic food is produced without the addition of any chemicals to the soil, crops or animals. Although organic foods are sometimes claimed to be safer and nutritionally superior to foods produced by non-organic methods, there has as yet been no certain scientific proof either way.

Chemicals in food processing

People have been adding substances to their food to improve its taste and appearance for hundreds of years. Salt, pepper, herbs, spices, sugar and honey are all natural ways of making food taste better. During the twentieth century, the proportion of food being cooked at home from fresh, raw ingredients decreased, and many people now rely heavily on convenience foods such as ready meals. Most convenience foods are prepared in huge batches and they are often stored for long periods. Manufacturers add various chemicals to ensure that these foods retain their freshness, appearance and flavour.

Flavour enhancers and preservatives

Flavour enhancers, such as salt, are added to bring out the flavour of food. Monosodium glutamate (MSG) is a common flavour enhancer that is added to processed foods.

Some sweets, like those in this photograph, are made using only natural colourings.

Preservatives are added to foods to prevent them 'going off'. The air is full of microbes, such as fungal spores and bacteria, and in a warm, moist atmosphere these microbes can easily grow on food and make it unsafe to eat. Preservatives prevent this happening. Two common preservatives are sorbic acid, which is widely used in drinks, dairy products, seafood and baked goods, and sulphur dioxide, which prevents bacterial growth and is used to preserve dried apricots, sausage meat and jams.

Colourings

As their name suggests, colourings add colour to a food. They might be added to a food that loses colour when it is cooked, such as marrowfat peas. They might also be added to make something look brighter and more attractive, to make a fruit drink look more orange, for example. Some colourings are natural; there is a red colouring that is made from the cochineal insect *Dactylopius coccus*. Others, like tartrazine (yellow) and amaranth (purple), are synthetic chemicals.

Ingredients: Glucose Syrup • Sugar • Strawberry, Blackcurrant, Lemon, Orange, Apple Juices (4.4%) • Hydrogenated Vegetable Oil • Citric Acid E330 • Gelatine • Egg White • Flavourings • Colours E104 E122 E110 E127 E132 E142 • Emulsifier E322.

This list of ingredients from a packet of chewy sweets shows that the sweets contain chemical colourings. Each colouring has an individual E number. E numbers are used throughout the processed food industry to identify chemical additives.

FOCUS

Sudan Red

In February 2005, hundreds of food products around the world were withdrawn from sale. They all contained a chemical called Sudan Red, a dye used in making oils, waxes and polishes that has been linked to an increased risk of cancer. The source of the contamination was found to be chilli powder which had been used in Worcester Sauce – itself an ingredient in a wide range of products. Graham Randall of Greggs, an English bakery company, said: "We were told by Premier Foods that this product was used in certain things ... they were instantly taken off the shelves and have not been on sale since..."

Emulsifiers and others

Emulsifiers help to stop the separation of ingredients such as oil and water. They are widely used in foods like ice cream, mayonnaise, margarine, bread, cakes and confectionery. A common emulsifier is lecithin, which is often made from soya beans or eggs. Gelling agents help to give food shape and structure, and prevent it from being runny. Pectin is a natural gelling agent used in making jams and jellies.

Thickeners help to thicken a food and are particularly useful in the production of low-fat and low-sugar foods. Stabilizers help to preserve the physical characteristics of a product. For example, they stop ice crystals forming in ice cream, and prevent oil and water separating in sauces and dressings. Stabilizers are vital ingredients in long-life dairy products such as yoghurts.

Benefits or risks?

This chapter has explored some of the ways in which chemicals end up in our foods. It has shown the types of chemicals that are added to foods, how they are added and why they are added. But why are some people unhappy about these added chemicals?

Chemicals and agriculture

Traces of chemicals sprayed onto crop plants during growth can still be present on the food we eat, and there is some evidence that these chemicals may be harmful to humans. Some chemicals can remain in the soil for many years, contaminating future crops. Chemical residues from vaccines, hormones and pesticides can remain in meat, milk and other animal products and thus enter the human food chain. There has also been concern in recent years that over-use of antibiotics in farm animals could lead to

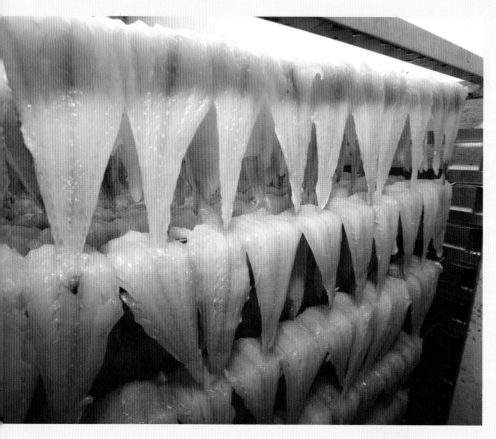

These smoked haddock fillets are ready to be packed. Their orange colour comes from a chemical dye, which is used to make them look more attractive.

the development of more antibiotic-resistant strains of microbes. This is because although most bacteria are killed when they are exposed to an antibiotic, a few stronger ones may survive and adapt to living with low levels of antibiotics, giving rise to 'resistant bacteria' that antibiotics cannot kill. The more antibiotics that are used, the more likely this is to happen.

To protect the public, samples of a wide range of foods are regularly tested by government agencies. Any that are found to contain dangerous chemical contamination or residue are withdrawn from sale and the source of the foods investigated to prevent a recurrence of the problem.

FORUM

Should we worry about the additives in our foods?

'The public should not be worried about additives because they have all been rigorously tested before they are allowed to be added to foods.'

Sarah Schenker, nutrition scientist for the British Nutrition Foundation, 1999

'I think we have got to the point now where it is no longer acceptable to continue to allow the food industry to add artificial colours to products deliberately targeted and marketed to babies and children.'

Erik Millstone, Professor of Science Policy at the University of Sussex, 2007

Do the benefits of adding chemicals to foods outweigh the possible risks?

Food additives

Some scientists think that certain food additives, like tartrazine, may be linked to behavioural problems in children, as well as to conditions including allergies, asthma and migraine. Other reports have linked saccharin to cancer in laboratory mice, and aspartame to changes in brain function. However, all food additives are tested rigorously before they are allowed to be added to foods. Any that are proven to be unsafe are banned.

Lack of knowledge

Although all chemicals are tested before they can be used on crops or animals, or added to foods during processing, some people think that we do not know enough about their possible long-term effects. It can be argued that chemicals now thought to be safe may in the future be found to be harmful.

Chapter 4

How do microbes affect our foods?

Microbes, or micro-organisms, are tiny living things that are too small to be seen with the naked eye. They include bacteria, viruses and fungi. Some microbes can themselves make food turn bad, while others release substances that can make people ill. Not all microbes in food are bad news – some are introduced on purpose and have beneficial effects!

FOCUS

E. coli outbreak

On 27 August 2006, Ruby Trautz, an 81-year-old woman from Nebraska, USA, was rushed to hospital. She was given morphine to relieve her pain, but there was little else doctors could do. She died four days later from a food-borne infection that was later identified as a virulent strain of *E. coli*. More cases followed, and by September it became apparent that there was a major outbreak of *E. coli* food poisoning. Scientists traced the source of the outbreak to fresh spinach, and suggested the bacteria may have been transferred to the spinach from contaminated water used for irrigation. At least 199 people in 28 states were infected, of whom 141 were taken to hospital and three died.

How do microbes get into our food?

Unwanted microbes get into our food in a variety of ways and contamination may occur at any stage. Most microbes require warmth and moisture to grow, but given these conditions they can multiply quickly in or on food.

An electron microscope was used to photograph these *Escherichia coli* bacteria. Some strains of *E. coli* can cause severe illness.

What effects do microbes have?

If we eat food contaminated by microbes, the microbes enter our bodies. Some cause food poisoning. The table shows five types of bacteria that are responsible for most cases of food poisoning.

Bacteria	Common sources	Effects	Special features
Campylobacter	Poultry, red meat Unpasteurized milk Untreated water	Severe diarrhoea Abdominal cramps	Does not grow in food but spreads easily
Clostridium perfringens	Meat and poultry, especially if slow-cooked and left to stand at room temperature	Nausea Diarrhoea Abdominal pain	Produces heat-resistant spores that are not destroyed by cooking
Salmonella	Unpasteurized milk, eggs, meat, poultry	Diarrhoea Abdominal cramps Nausea Vomiting Headaches	Can survive in undercooked food, and can continue to multiply unless chilled
Listeria	Many types of food, especially unwashed vegetables and soft mould-ripened cheeses and pâtés	Severe illness in vulnerable people such as pregnant women, babies and the elderly	Killed by pasteurization and cooking
Escherichia coli (E. coli)	Undercooked meat Unpasteurized milk	Diarrhoea Abdominal cramps, in severe cases kidney failure and even death	The strains responsible for the most serious outbreaks produce a chemical called verocytotoxin

Although bacteria are the main source of food poisoning, some viruses are dangerous too. For example, Calicivirus (also called Norwalk-like virus), causes acute vomiting and diarrhoea. This virus spreads from one infected person to another, so food can be contaminated if handled by infected workers.

Why are microbes added to some foods?

Microbes that are added to our foods intentionally include:

- ***baking yeast*** A type of fungus that makes bread and other doughs rise.

- ***moulds*** Some cheeses, such as blue Stilton and Roquefort, are intentionally infected with specific moulds to add flavour and colouring.

- ***bacteria*** Some products that are labelled as 'probiotic' contain bacteria that can help the digestive system to function well.

The characteristic blue colouring of this Stilton cheese is due to the deliberate growth of mould in the cheese.

Microbes and crops

Microbes are all around us, in air, soil, water, people and animals, and on most surfaces. Microbes can be transferred to fruit, vegetables and other crops from many different sources. The soil in which a crop is grown may contain microbes from previous plants. Water used for irrigation or to wash a crop may be contaminated. Wild, farm or domestic animals that come close to crops may transfer microbes to the plants. Machinery and other equipment used in harvesting a crop may be contaminated.

In order to minimize the risk of microbial contamination of crops, most producers follow rigorous guidelines. Many fresh fruits and vegetables also have their own natural barrier, such as skin or peel, which reduces the likelihood of microbes reaching the edible parts inside.

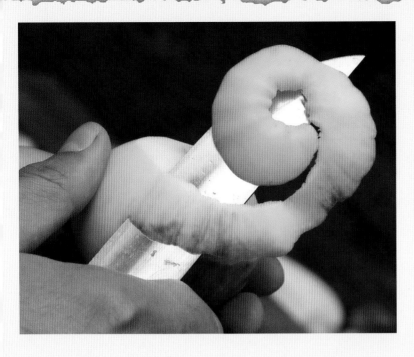

The skin of this apple acts as a natural barrier to microbes.

Microbes and animals

Microbes can infect farm animals. In many cases the animal itself does not fall sick, but the microbes remain in the animal's products – eggs, milk or meat – which are then consumed by humans. Farm animals can become infected through their environment, for example from contact with other infected animals or their waste, or with contaminated feed or water, equipment, machinery or workers. Most farmers are extremely careful to prevent any infections arising in their livestock.

Prions

Prions are proteins (not microbes) that can cause brain and nervous system diseases including bovine spongeiform encaphilitis (BSE, or 'mad cow disease') in cows, and scrapie in sheep and goats. Although scrapie has not been found to infect humans, the BSE prion can infect humans, causing Creutzfeldt-Jakob disease. Scientists do not fully understand how prion diseases are contracted or spread but it has been suggested that contaminated feedstuffs may be one source of infection of farm animals.

Expert View

'The public generally perceives agricultural residues, pesticides and veterinary drugs as the major sources of health risks, but they are not. In Europe, for example, they account for just 0.5 per cent of foodborne illnesses. More common, and possibly increasing in frequency, is contamination by bacteria, protozoa, parasites, viruses and fungi or their toxins, introduced during food handling.'

FAO factsheet,
'Food quality and safety' 2001

Microbes in food processing and storage

Many food crops, and some animal products such as eggs, are packaged on the farms where they are produced and then transported to retailers or directly to users. Others are transported to factories or processing plants. However, both fresh foods and processed foods are stored before being bought and eaten, and microbes can contaminate the foods at any stage. For example, microbes can be transferred to a food from contaminated workers or equipment, or from one food to another – called 'cross-contamination'. Food producers, packagers, transporters and retailers take great care to prevent any contamination.

Strict hygiene precautions are taken at food processing plants such as this one where milk is bottled. Most milk is pasteurized before bottling, which kills any microbes present.

In June 2006, Cadbury Schweppes detected tiny amounts of salmonella in some of its chocolate products. The company told the Food Standards Agency, the regulating authority in the United Kingdom, about the problem. It also recalled more than one million chocolate bars from shops and issued a press release advising people not to eat any bars they may already have bought. An investigation suggested that the source of the outbreak was a leaking pipe at the Cadbury Schweppes factory in Herefordshire. Altogether, 37 people were reported to have become ill as a result of eating the infected chocolate – and the incident may have cost Cadbury Schweppes more than £20 million in profits.

Hygiene

In most developed countries, strict rules are in force to minimize the chances of food becoming contaminated with microbes during processing and storage. The problems are much greater in poorer countries, however, where political, social and environmental circumstances often make it impossible to maintain high standards of hygiene.

These girls in Mali have only muddy river water to wash their dishes in, but washing and cleaning in dirty water can lead to infections from parasites, bacteria or other microbes.

Are microbes a serious risk in our food?

Although microbial contamination of our food is always possible, there are steps that can be taken to minimize the risks to human health. Food producers, processors and packagers reduce the risk of contamination by thorough cleaning of equipment and premises, and by maintaining good hygiene standards for their workers. Keeping different types of food apart also helps to prevent cross-contamination.

Most microbes need warmth and moisture to multiply. Storing foods at low temperatures in a refrigerator or freezer prevents microbes from growing. Some foods, such as pulses, are dried for storage to prevent microbe growth. Vinegar, used for pickling, also prevents microbe growth, as does salt.

Expert View

'Microbial contamination is commonplace where hygiene is poor, frequently because of lack of access to clean water. It is a major source of illness, especially among children.'

FAO factsheet,
'Food quality and safety' 2001

Killing microbes

The high temperatures of heat treatments like pasteurization kill any microbes present. Other methods for killing microbes include the use of irradiation and ultraviolet light. Irradiation damages the DNA of any microbes that are in the food. This means that the microbes are unable to multiply and so the food is safe to eat. There are three different technologies that can be used to irradiate food, and the table shows the advantages and disadvantages of each method.

Irradiation method	Advantages	Disadvantages
Gamma rays	Can penetrate deeply so they can be used to treat thick foods.	Heavy protective shielding is needed. The radioactive source has to be stored safely when not in use.
Electron beam	No heavy shielding is needed. Can be switched off when not in use.	Cannot penetrate more than 3 cm so can only be used to treat thin foods.
X-rays	Can penetrate deeply so they can be used to treat thick foods. Can be switched off when not in use.	Heavy protective shielding is needed.

At home

There are steps that individuals can and should take to minimize the risk of contracting a food-borne microbial infection. Remember the four key words – the four 'C's:

1 **Clean** Keep your hands, utensils and cooking area clean at all times.
2 **Cook** Make sure all food is thoroughly cooked right through.
3 **Chill** Avoid leaving fresh produce and leftover food at room temperature – put it in the fridge straightaway.
4 **don't Cross-contaminate** Wash your hands and any utensils after they have been in contact with food and before they touch another food. Keep raw meat and cooked meats apart.

In this refrigerator, the raw meat (left) and cooked meat (right) are stored on separate plates. Both plates are wrapped. These measures can help to prevent bacterial contamination that could lead to food poisoning.

If you do contract a foodborne microbial infection, reduce the risk of it spreading by avoiding contact with vulnerable people. Reporting the outbreak to your doctor or local public health department is also advisable.

FORUM

Do individuals know enough about the risks to avoid microbial contamination of their food, and do they act on this information?

'With busy lifestyles, we know food safety isn't always [at the] top of [people's] mind[s], so FDF [the Food and Drink Federation] is working hard with schools, local authorities and businesses across the UK to raise awareness of the "follow the 4 Cs message" to help people continue to enjoy and keep their food safe once it's left the shop shelf.'

Melanie Leech, Director General, Food and Drink Federation, 2006

'The best news about food safety is that one doesn't have to be a rocket scientist to do it properly. The bad news is that even a simple and obvious thing like hand washing – which protects incredibly well – is seen by many people as good health theory, but not actually put into practise.'

Hugh Pennington, Professor of Microbiology at Aberdeen University, 2003

Do you practice good food hygiene?

Chapter 5

How can we know if our food is safe?

It might seem that hidden dangers lurk in every mouthful of food! But the fact that there *could* be a risk does not mean there actually is a danger. Governments have set up strict checks and guidelines at every stage, from the farm to your fork, to make sure your food is safe to eat.

Government regulations

Different countries have different regulations and different authorities to enforce them, but they all have a very similar aim: to minimize the risk of any foodborne illness. In the United States, the Food and Drug Administration (FDA), together with Centers for Disease Control and Prevention (CDC), the U.S. Department of Agriculture (USDA) and the Environmental Protection Agency (EPA), cover every aspect of food safety. In the United Kingdom food issues are regulated by the Food Standards Agency (FSA), together with other government departments such as the Department for the Environment, Farming and Rural Affairs (DEFRA). It is the task of these agencies to decide whether or not to approve a new genetically modified food. They oversee the testing and approval of chemical additives and new technologies. They are responsible for inspecting food imported from countries where food regulations may be different. Inspectors from these agencies also inspect premises to check on microbial contamination and any other food hazards.

Expert View

'As a microbiologist, I set out to investigate how irradiation can not only kill harmful bacteria that causes food poisoning in humans but also how it can destroy spoilage bacteria and so offer longer shelf life to food products. ... Without a doubt, food irradiation is a real benefit for the consumer. I often compare it to pasteurization – both prevent food spoilage while at the same time killing harmful bacteria.'

Dr. Margaret Patterson, food scientist at Queens University in Belfast, 2002

The strawberries on the left were irradiated after they were picked. This killed any microbes on or in them, keeping them fresh for longer. The strawberries on the right were not irradiated and are clearly not fit to eat.

New technologies

New technologies that could make our food even safer are tested and, when found to be beneficial, become standard within the food industry. One technology makes use of ozone gas to react with certain chemicals inside microbes. The reaction ruptures the cell walls of the microbes, thus killing them. Other technologies include new anti-microbial washes and anti-bacterial sprays, improved testing techniques and food irradiation. However, some people remain concerned that irradiated food may not be safe. When food is irradiated, chemicals called 'unique radiolytic products' (URPs) are formed. Some people think that these URPs may be harmful to humans. The rules about food irradiation differ from one country to another; some countries allow many irradiated foods while others restrict the process to a few food types.

Controlling, checking and testing

Food hygiene inspectors carry out regular inspections of all types of premises involved in the production of food, including farms, factories, abbatoirs, shops, restaurants and school kitchens. An inspector needs to find out whether adequate hygiene standards are maintained, whether the food produced is safe to eat, and whether food poisoning or other injury might occur as a consequence of eating the food.

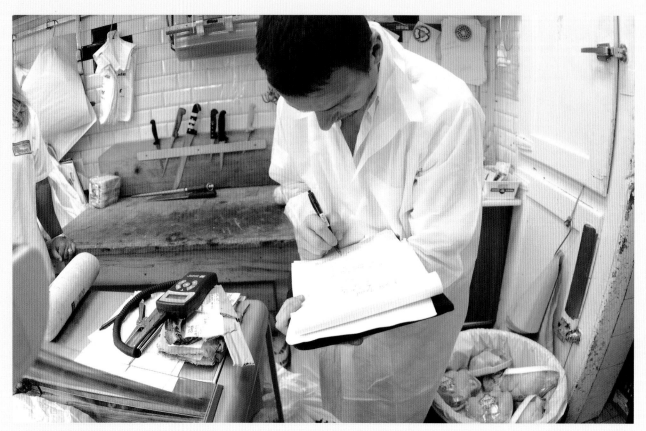

A health inspector in France notes down his observations after an inspection of a deep freeze at a butcher's shop.

Some of the things that an inspector looks at include:

• *Management* A manager should know about any hazards in his or her business, and should have set up systems to ensure that those hazards do not result in the contamination of food. Managers should also monitor every aspect of the business closely, and have written records to prove that they have done so.

• *Staff training* All staff should have had proper training for the job they are employed to do, such as food hygiene training. Within the business, each member of staff should know exactly what his or her responsibilities are, so that vital checks do not get overlooked.

- **Temperature control** Temperatures of fridges and freezers should be checked and recorded regularly, and foods such as meat should be checked to make sure they are thoroughly cooked.

- **Cleanliness** All surfaces and equipment should be clean.

- **Avoiding cross-contamination** Raw and cooked foods should be stored and prepared separately

- **Staff hygiene** All staff should have high standards of personal hygiene and wear suitable clean clothing. There should be adequate facilities for staff to wash their hands frequently and easily.

- **Pests** There should be no signs of any pests such as flies, mice or cockroaches on the premises.

After an inspection

After an inspection, the inspector writes a report giving details of what he or she observed at the premises. The manager of the premises is given a copy, and a copy is kept by the authorities. The report may contain recommendations of action to be taken to improve a particular aspect of the business. If this is the case, there will be a follow-up inspection to check that the recommendations have been carried out. If an inspector finds something that is considered a danger to the public, the business can be closed immediately.

Expert View

These are extracts from genuine food hygiene inspectors' reports:

'During my inspection, I was informed joints of meat are cooled down for between six to seven hours within the kitchen before being placed within the fridge. This practice is unsafe and must stop.'

'During my initial visit dead cockroaches were found in traps in the kitchen. Cockroach activity in a hospital kitchen in particular poses a risk to health and is not acceptable.'

Reported by Andrew Dagnell, **Wales On Sunday, 2007**

Informing and acting

The information from scientific tests, safety checks and inspections is examined closely to decide whether any action needs to be taken. For example, if scientific analysis of a product shows that it contains a prohibited substance, government agencies will ensure that the product is immediately withdrawn from sale to the public. Alerts will be issued in newspapers and on radio and television to warn the public of the potential risk. An investigation will be undertaken to discover how the problem occurred, and the company involved may be fined or prosecuted.

Swift action is also taken if a number of people in one area all contract a foodborne illness at the same time. Details are collected of the foods they have eaten, and where the foods came from, to try to find any common factors that may lead to the source of the outbreak. A retailer or restaurant can be closed immediately if the outbreak is traced back to them.

Food inspectors test cooked burger meat in a fast-food restaurant.

Food labelling

Information about individual food items is provided on its packaging. Food labelling gives a huge amount of information about what the food product contains, how it should be stored and cooked, and the date before which it should be eaten. There are strict rules about this labelling. For example, in the United States and the UK a full list of ingredients must appear, together with an analysis of the food's nutritional content. Any ingredient that is known as a common cause of allergy, such as nuts, must be clearly labelled. If the food contains GM products, or has been irradiated, this must also be clearly indicated. Storage instructions, durability and cooking instructions must be shown. The packaging must not contain anything untrue that might mislead the public.

A global issue

As much of our food is imported from other countries, food safety is no longer an issue that can be dealt with by individual countries working alone. Instead, a more global approach is evolving, with countries sharing information and working together to improve food safety standards worldwide. For example, the World Health Organization published a Global Strategy for Food Safety in 2002 and set up The International Food Safety Authorities Network (INFOSAN) to improve international communication about food safety issues. The Food and Agriculture Organization (FAO) of the United Nations is involved in global food safety and the European Food Safety Authority (EFSA) oversees issues within the European Union.

A scientist examines a chicken egg at a research facility that advises the Belgian food safety agency.

FORUM

Are current measures sufficient to ensure our food is safe?

' ... the current inspection of food is antiquated and incapable of keeping up with the changes in the way food is produced, distributed and consumed. Food-borne illness seems to be on the rise and new disease-causing microbes continue to appear.'

David A. Kessler, Food and Drug Administration Commissioner, 2008

'... WHO works closely with the Food and Agriculture Organization of the United Nations (FAO) to address food safety issues along the entire food production chain – from production to consumption – using new methods of risk analysis. These methods provide efficient, science-based tools to improve food safety, thereby benefiting both public health and economic development.'

World Health Organization website 'Food safety'

What do you think?

Chapter 6

What will the future bring?

The newspapers, television and radio frequently report news about food scares that make people anxious. Issues about food safety are likely to continue to have a high profile in the media because it is a subject that concerns everyone. But it should be remembered that the risk to the individual is often far lower than the headlines might suggest.

Increased demand

As the population of our planet increases, so does the demand for food. This puts farmers under increasing pressure to produce higher yields from the land. As countries develop and their economies grow, individuals become better off and their consumption of meat increases. A meat-based diet requires much more land than a plant-based diet because animals do not convert plant material into edible meat efficiently: one person eating a plant-based diet needs about one-fifth of the amount of food that livestock need to provide meat for one person for a year. Global issues such as these will affect the types of food we eat and their production, and so may ultimately affect the safety of our food.

These people are waiting for food aid distribution in Maikona, Kenya. Like many people in this region, they have lost most of their animals in a devastating drought and would face starvation without this aid. The challenge for the future is how to end their dependence on this donated food.

This scientist is working to preserve the heritage and diversity of crops and vegetables, and to improve their flavour, yield and resistance to disease.

The demand for organic food has increased steadily in recent years and current indications are that this trend will continue. It has been suggested, however, that avoiding the use of chemicals during production and processing may increase the risk of some foodborne microbial diseases. Some organic farmers avoid using modern agrochemicals by reverting to traditional remedies, which may actually be more harmful to the consumer and the environment than the modern replacement. Supporters of the organic food movement argue that these risks are small compared with those of non-organic food.

Some people suggest that GM foods hold the key to our future food needs. Planting GM crops reduces pesticide and herbicide use, while at the same time increasing crop yield and allowing cultivation of previously unsuitable land. Others, though, warn of the potential dangers of the rapid expansion of a technology whose long-term effects cannot yet be known. While GM food may provide solutions to future problems, it may also pose as yet unknown risks.

Food miles

Some foods now have pictures of aeroplanes on the packaging to indicate that they have been transported by air. Many people are concerned about the amount of produce being air-freighted around the world because of the resulting carbon dioxide emissions from aeroplanes. The amount of food being flown into the UK, for example, doubled during the 1990s. One solution is to try to buy more locally sourced food with fewer 'food miles'. Another possibility is for food imports to travel by other, less polluting, ways, such as in cargo ships. However, the increased journey times involved would require new methods of keeping the food fresh for longer, which raises more issues about food safety.

Expert View

'Recent trends in global food production, processing, distribution and preparation are creating an increasing demand for food safety research in order to ensure a safer global food supply.'

WHO website 'Food safety'

Medicine in your food?

Scientists are continually searching for ways to make our food safer. These are just some of the new technologies that are under investigation and which may soon appear in the food production lines or on our supermarket shelves.

Genetic engineers have created a variety of tomato that produces HIV (Human Immunodeficiency Virus) and HBV (Hepatitis B virus) proteins. When the tomatoes are eaten, the proteins stimulate an immune response in the same way as other oral vaccines, thus offering protection against infection. It is possible that other medicines could be introduced into food in this way. However, it could be difficult to control the amount of medicine an individual receives so, for more accurate dosage measurement, these foods may be grown and then made into tablets or capsules.

FORUM

Will our food be safe in the future?

'The global community must keep its sights set on the goal of assuring food security for all. Condemning biotechnology for its potential risks without considering the alternative risks of prolonging the human misery caused by hunger, malnutrition, and child death is unwise and unethical. In a world where the consequence of inaction is death of thousands of children, we must not ignore any part of a possible solution, including agricultural biotechnology...'

Per Pinstrup-Andersen, Director General, International Food Policy Research Institute, 2001

'There have been many food and public health scandals in Europe over the past few years – mad cow disease in the UK, dioxins in Belgian chicken feed, tainted blood in France – and these have left a strong impression in the public's mind, which is that politicians, scientists, doctors and the food industry are not to be trusted.'

Conference Report, **International Conference Perspectives for Food 2030,** *Brussels, 2007*

What do you think?

Is it ripe?

It can be difficult to tell whether fruit is ripe or not. New stickers are being produced that detect ethylene, a gas given off by fruit as it ripens. When the fruit is ripe, the sticker changes colour. This will make it easier to choose ripe fruit without squeezing and possibly damaging it.

Nanotechnology

Nanotechnology is a relatively new and exciting branch of science that works at the level of individual molecules. On this incredibly tiny scale the normal rules of physics do not apply, so incorporating nanotechnology into a product gives it new properties. Some food-related nanotechnology products are already available and others are being developed. Nanotechnology seems set to affect our food safety in many different ways.

Products available already, although still undergoing further development, include:

- nano-coated packaging to sense microbial and biochemical changes in the food. On detecting a change, the packaging reacts either by changing colour to warn the food is unsafe to eat, or by releasing a chemical to make it safe.
- kitchen utensils and containers coated with an anti-microbial nano-coating that detects bacterial contamination and reacts to combat infection.
- nanoparticles on items such as cooking pots to increase properties such as heat conduction.
- nanoparticles embedded inside food to carry medicines or nutrients into the body without changing the taste of the food.

Nanotechnology has many possible applications in the food industry. This computer artwork shows nanorobots attacking and killing a *Salmonella* bacterium.

Research is still being carried out on other products including:

- in agriculture, nanosensors that can be distributed across fields to monitor soil conditions and crop growth, and to automatically detect, locate, and report findings, and apply water, fertilizers and pesticides.
- nano herbicides and pesticides that are more stable, more toxic to pests and more easily absorbed by plants than existing chemicals.

Glossary

additive A substance that is added to food.

allergy A reaction to a particular substance.

antibiotic Medicine taken to cure an infection.

asthma A condition that can cause breathing difficulties.

bacterium (plural: bacteria) A type of microbe that can cause infections.

cell One of the tiny building blocks from which all living things are made.

chromosome One of the thread-like structures that carry genetic information.

cochineal A red food colouring obtained from insects.

contaminate To mix with something and spoil it.

DNA (deoxyribose nucleic acid) A molecule found in chromosomes.

E. coli A bacterium that causes foodborne infections.

emulsifier A chemical that is added to foods to prevent the separation of ingredients.

enzyme A chemical that is biologically active.

fertilizer A chemical that is added to plants to promote growth.

gelling agent A substance that is added to foods to make them less runny.

genetic code The set of information that controls everything about an organism.

genetic engineering A technique used to alter the genetic code of an organism.

genetic modification The process of using genetic engineering to alter a genetic code.

genome The complete genetic code of an organism.

herbicide A chemical that is used to kill weeds.

hormone A biological chemical that affects body functions such as growth.

irradiate To subject something to radiation.

lecithin A chemical that is used as an emulsifier.

mercury A metallic element that can be harmful to human and animal health.

microbe A living organism that is too small to be seen with the naked eye.

nanotechnology The field of science that works with individual molecules.

organic Describes something that is grown without artificial chemicals.

pasteurization A high-temperature method of killing microbes in milk.

pectin A substance that is added to foods to make them less runny.

pesticide A chemical used to kill pests.

pharmacological Describes something to do with medicines.

plasmid A ring of DNA found in some bacteria.

preservative Substance added to foods to prevent them going bad.

prion A chemical that can cause diseases such as BSE.

saccharin A synthetic sweetener.

salmonella Bacterium that can cause foodborne infections.

sterile Free of microbes.

synthetic Something that is made by humans rather than occurring naturally.

toxin A poisonous chemical.

vaccine A chemical that protects against contracting a particular infection.

virus A type of microbe.

Further information

Books
In the News: Food Safety and Farming by Angela Smith, Franklin Watts, 2002

Diseases and People: Food Poisoning and Foodborne Diseases by Sara L. Latta, Enslow Publishers, 1999

What's in Your Food? Recipe for Disaster: Processed Food by Paula Johanson, Rosen Central, 2008

Body Story: Spreading Menace: Salmonella Attack and the Hunger Craving by Elaine Pascoe, Blackbirch Press, 2003

Ideas & Inventions: Food and Farming: Feeding an Expanding World by Philip Wilkinson, Chrysalis Children's Books, 2005

Websites
www.agr.state.nc.us/cyber/kidswrld/foodsafe/index.htm
   Fun website that provides plenty of information about food safety.

www.eufic.org
   Click on the Food Safety and Quality tab.
   The website of the European Food Information Council provides information about food safety and quality.

www.eatwell.gov.uk/keepingfoodsafe/
   The Food Standards Agency site provides advice about how to keep your food safe.

www.foodfuture.org.uk
   Here you will find a discussion about the advantages and disadvantages of GM food.

Index

Entries in **bold** are for pictures.